The Artistry
George Shearing

MW00379362

Solo Piano Transcriptions by Bob Hinz

Project Manager: Tony Esposito
Production Coordinator: Hank Fields

Contents

HAPPINESS IS A THING CALLED JOE

Music by HAROLD ARLEN
Lyric by E.Y. HARBURG

Happiness Is a Thing Called Joe – 5 – 1
AFM00018

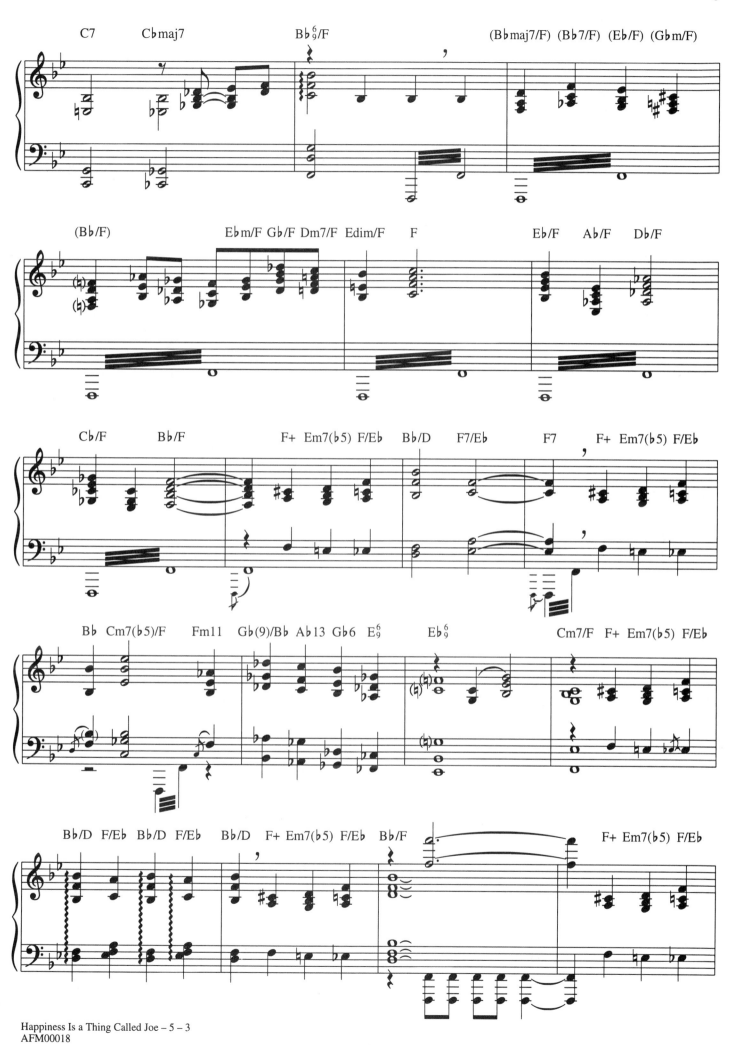

6

CHILDREN'S WALTZ

By GEORGE SHEARING

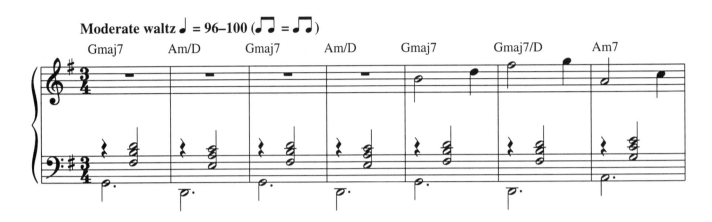

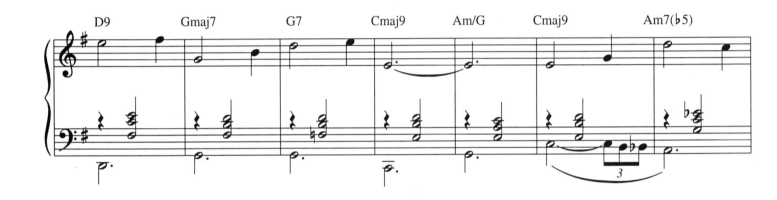

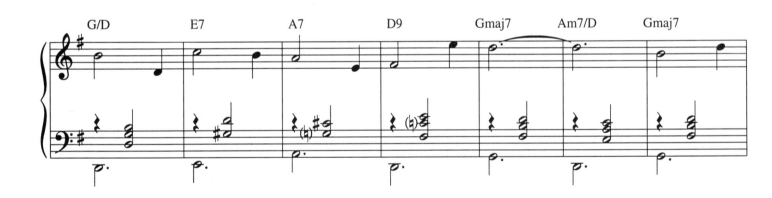

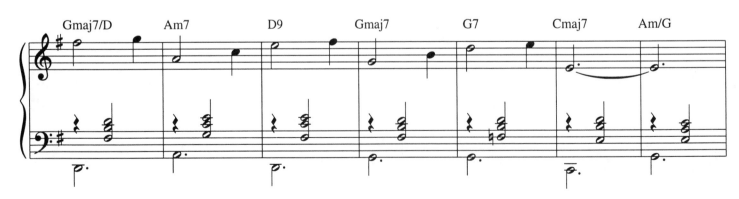

Children's Waltz – 4 – 1
AFM00018

Children's Waltz – 4 – 2
AFM00018

FOR YOU

Words by AL DUBIN
Music by JOE BURKE

For You – 9 – 1
AFM00018

14

For You – 9 – 3
AFM00018

16

For You – 9 – 5
AFM00018

18

For You – 9 – 7
AFM00018

For You – 9 – 8
AFM00018

20

For You – 9 – 9
AFM00018

IT HAD TO BE YOU

Words by GUS KAHN
Music by ISHAM JONES

It Had to Be You – 9 – 1
AFM00018

It Had to Be You – 9 – 3
AFM00018

It Had to Be You – 9 – 6
AFM00018

28

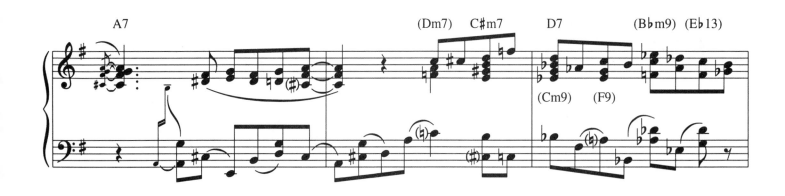

It Had to Be You – 9 – 8
AFM00018

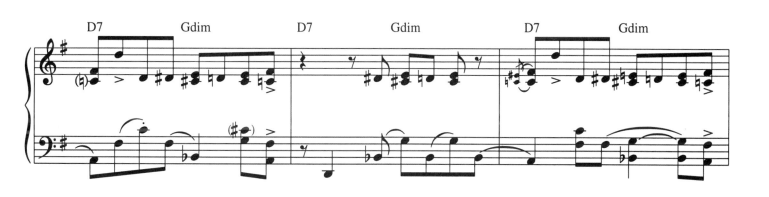

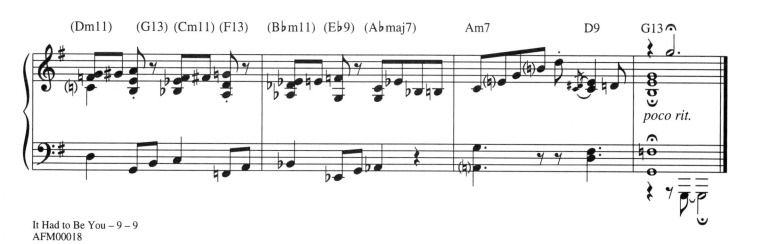

It Had to Be You – 9 – 9
AFM00018

IT'S YOU OR NO ONE

Words by SAMMY CAHN
Music by JULE STYNE

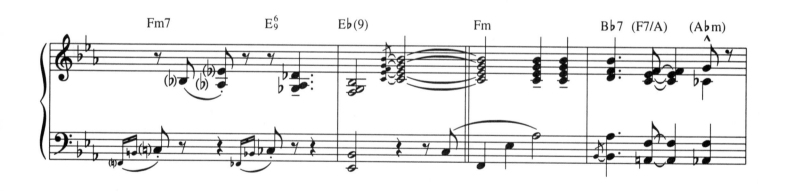

It's You or No One – 7 – 1
AFM00018

It's You or No One – 7 – 2
AFM00018

32

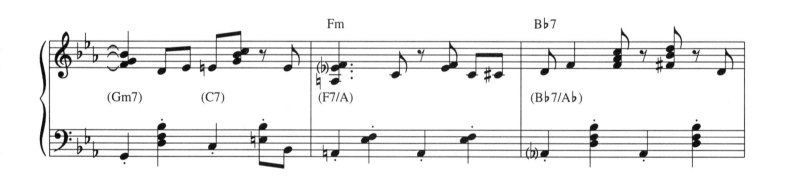

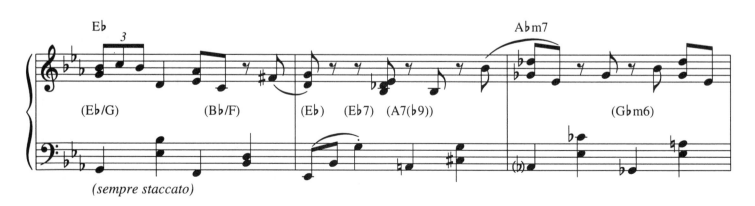

It's You or No One – 7 – 3
AFM00018

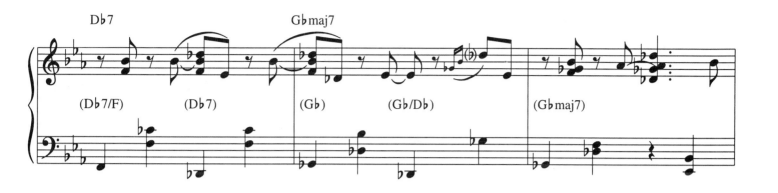

It's You or No One – 7 – 4
AFM00018

34

It's You or No One – 7 – 5
AFM00018

It's You or No One – 7 – 6
AFM00018

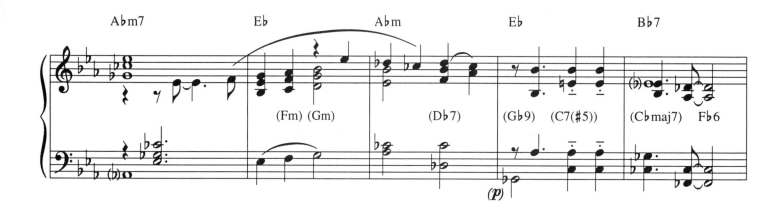

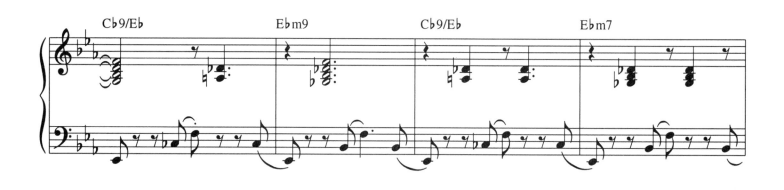

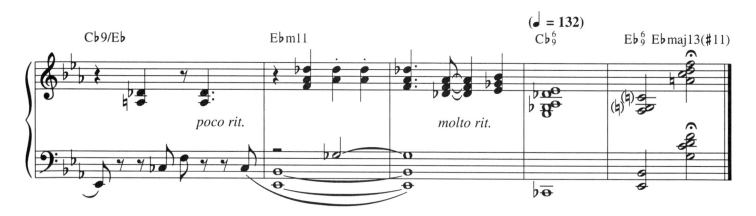

It's You or No One – 7 – 7

AFM00018

JOHN O'GROATS

By ALLAN CLAIRE
Arranged by GEORGE SHEARING

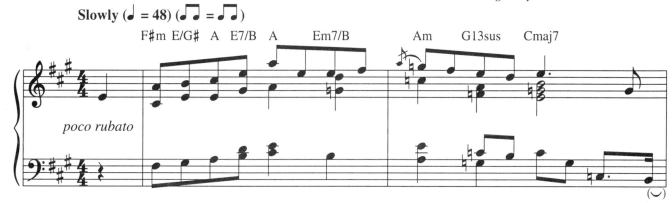

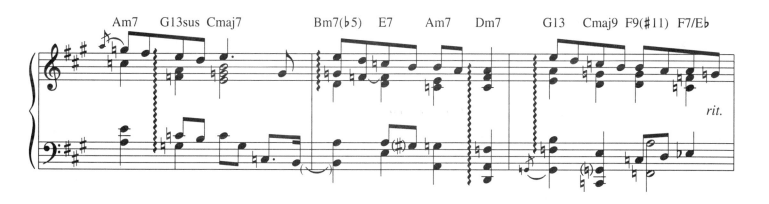

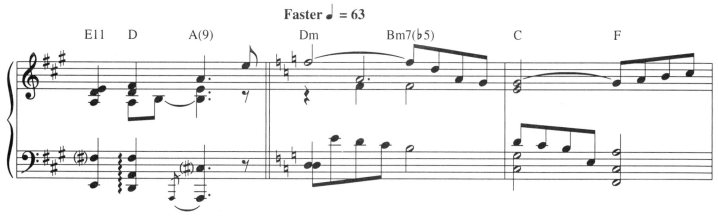

John O'Groats – 3 – 1
AFM00018

38

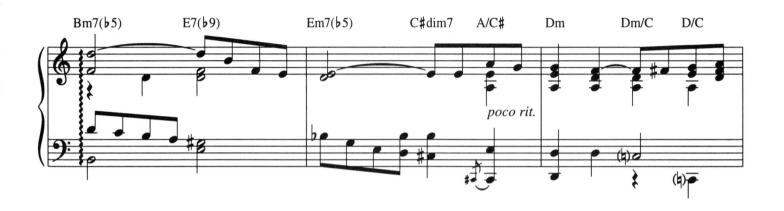

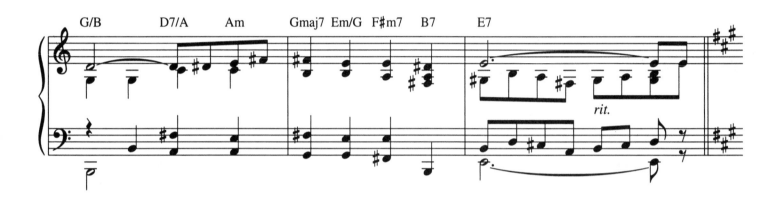

Tempo primo ♩ = 48

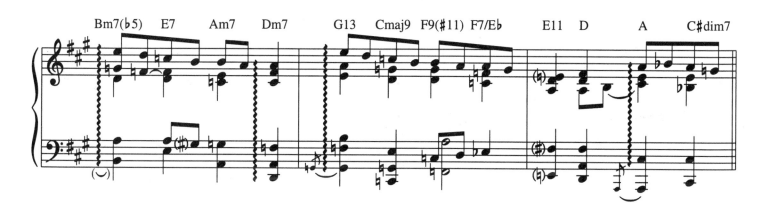

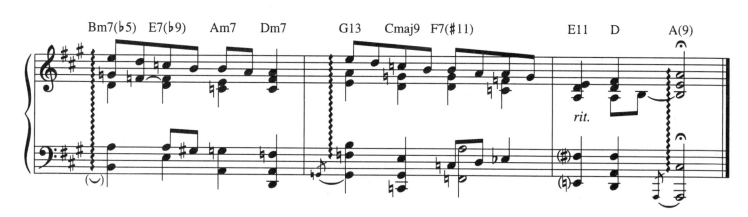

John O'Groats – 3 – 3
AFM00018

MISS INVISIBLE

By BOB HABER
and RON KAEHLER

Miss Invisible – 7 – 1
AFM00018

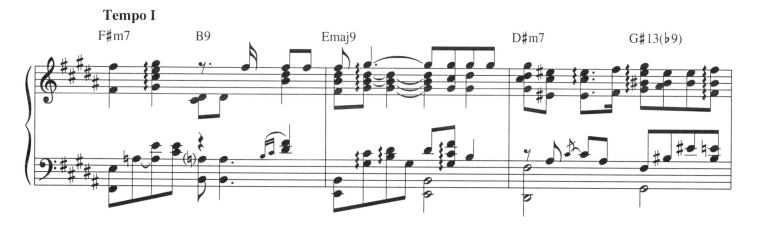

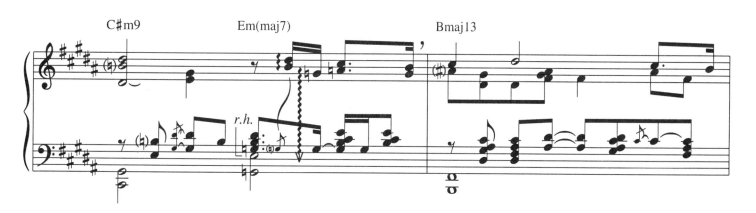

42

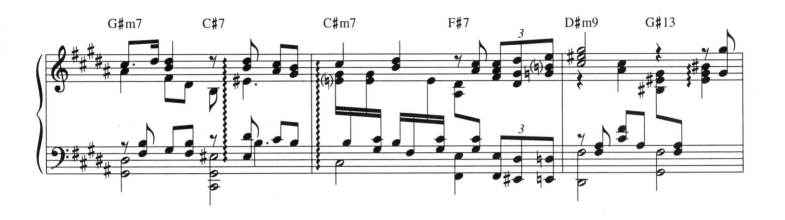

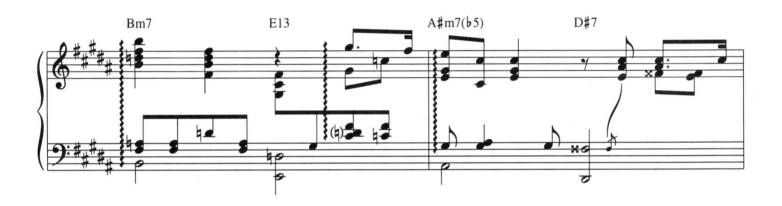

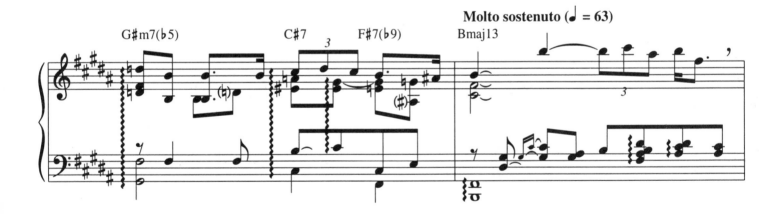

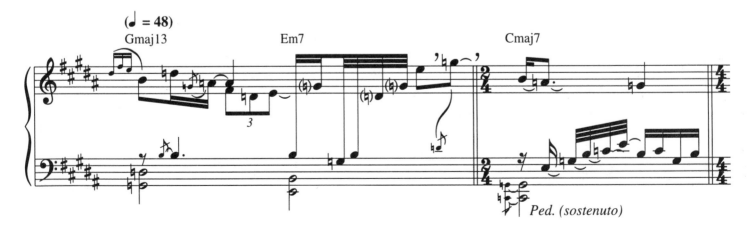

Miss Invisible – 7 – 3
AFM00018

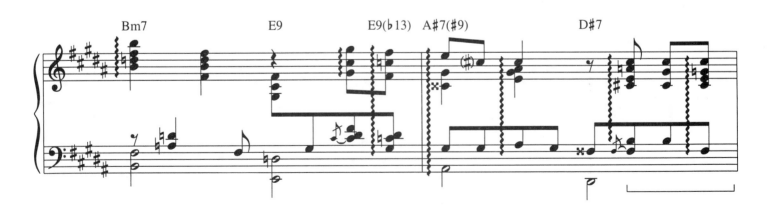

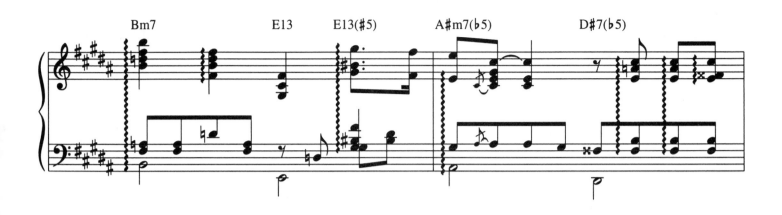

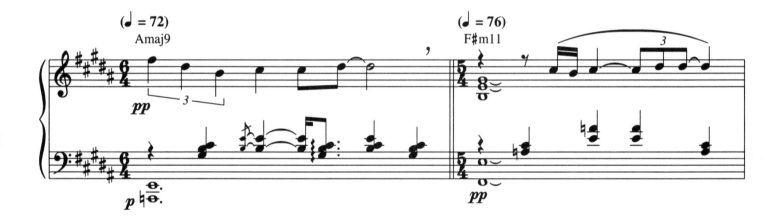

THINKING OF YOU

Words by BERT KALMAR
Music by HARRY RUBY

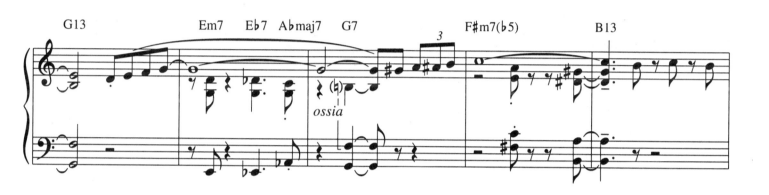

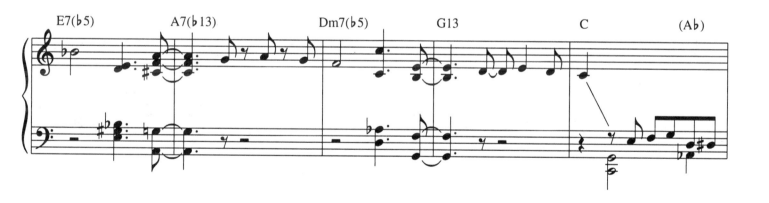

Thinking of You – 7 – 1
AFM00018

48

Thinking of You – 7 – 2
AFM00018

50

Thinking of You – 7 – 4

AFM00018

52

WALTZ FOR CLAUDIA

By KEVIN GIBBS

56

Faster (♩ = 160) Giusto (in strict time)

Waltz for Claudia – 6 – 3
AFM00018

58

Waltz for Claudia – 6 – 5
AFM00018

WENDY

By GEORGE SHEARING

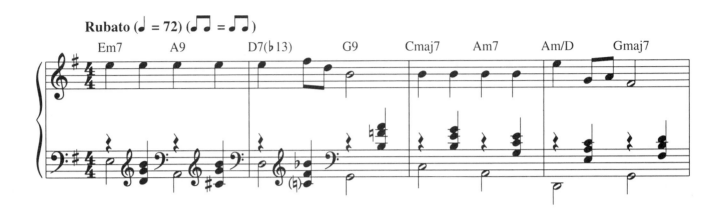

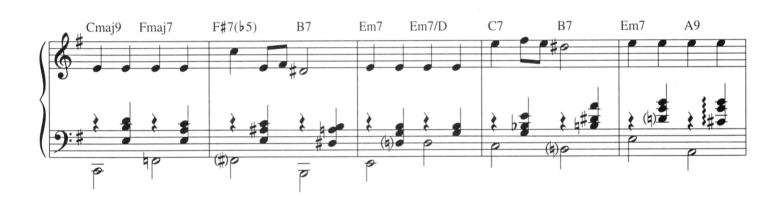

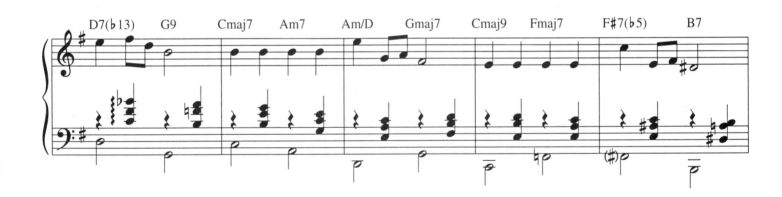

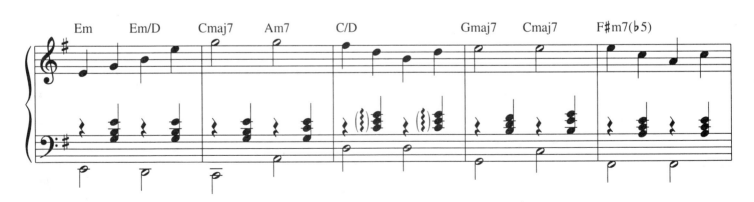

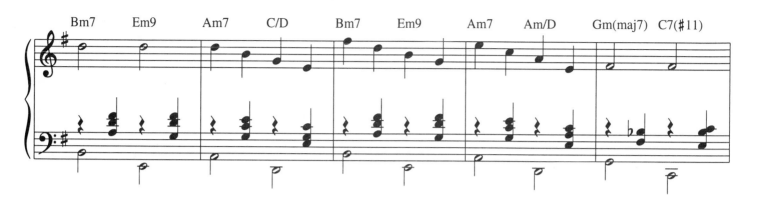

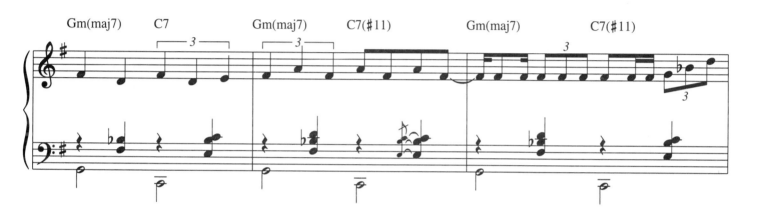

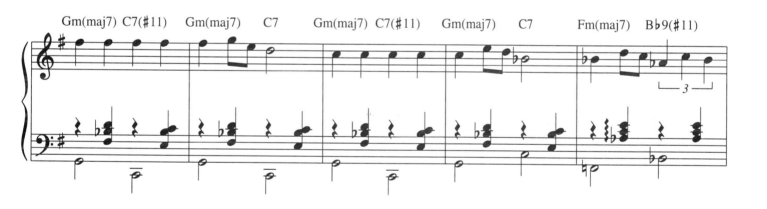

62

Wendy – 4 – 3
AFM00018

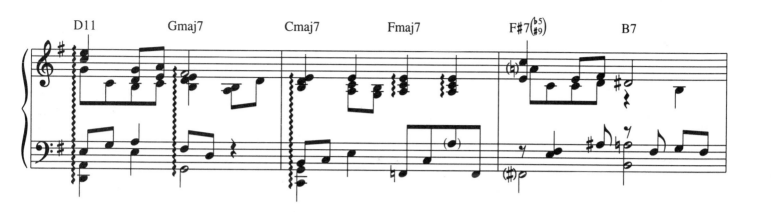

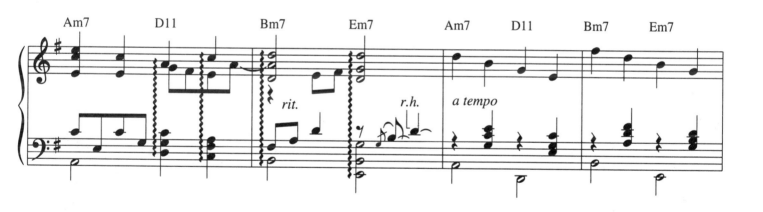

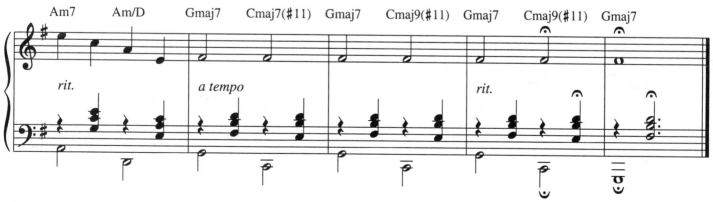

Wendy – 4 – 4
AFM00018

YOU'RE MY EVERYTHING

Lyrics by MORT DIXON and JOE YOUNG
Music by HARRY WARREN

Rubato

You're My Everything – 8 – 1
AFM00018

66

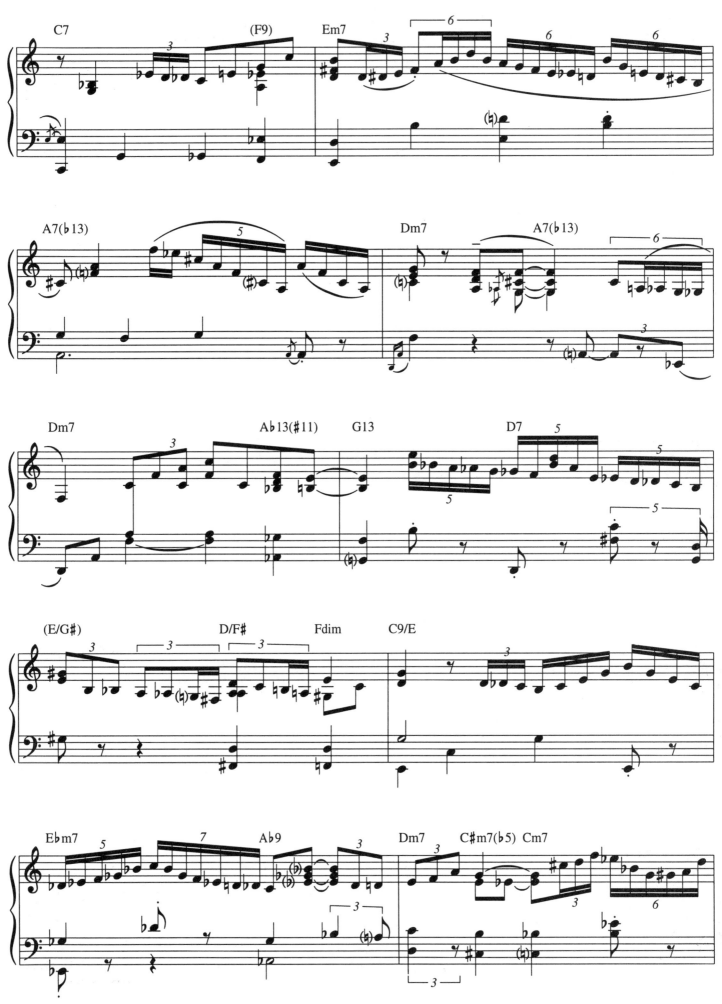

You're My Everything – 8 – 3
AFM00018

68

You're My Everything – 8 – 6
AFM00018

70

You're My Everything – 8 – 7
AFM00018

You're My Everything – 8 – 8
AFM00018